The Cup in the Master's Hand

Genesis V. Salmon

ISBN 978-1-68570-670-8 (paperback)
ISBN 979-8-88832-611-4 (hardcover)
ISBN 978-1-68570-671-5 (digital)

Christian Faith Publishing
832 Park Avenue
Meadville, PA 16335
www.christianfaithpublishing.com

Printed in the United States of America

To my mother, Anabel Venegas, for being an example of a true vessel of God. Thank you for praying and helping to mold me from a miry clay to a cup in the Master's hands (Psalm 40:1–3).

Hi! I'm Clay, but the potter isn't finished with me yet. I can't wait to see what I'll become!

I know I'll be in the palace, but what I become, I'll have to wait and see!

I dream of being a flower vase and maybe catching a glimpse of the Master as He walks into the room.

Maybe I'll be the pitcher that holds the water used to water the Master's flowers. I can't even begin to imagine!

Here I go: spin, mold, cut, bake. Ta-da! What am I?

As the potter holds up the mirror, I see what I am.

I shout with joy, "**I AM A CUP!**" I will be a cup in the Master's palace!

As I'm being delivered to the palace, I can only imagine how amazing it will be. I can't help but wonder if I will get to see the other cups.

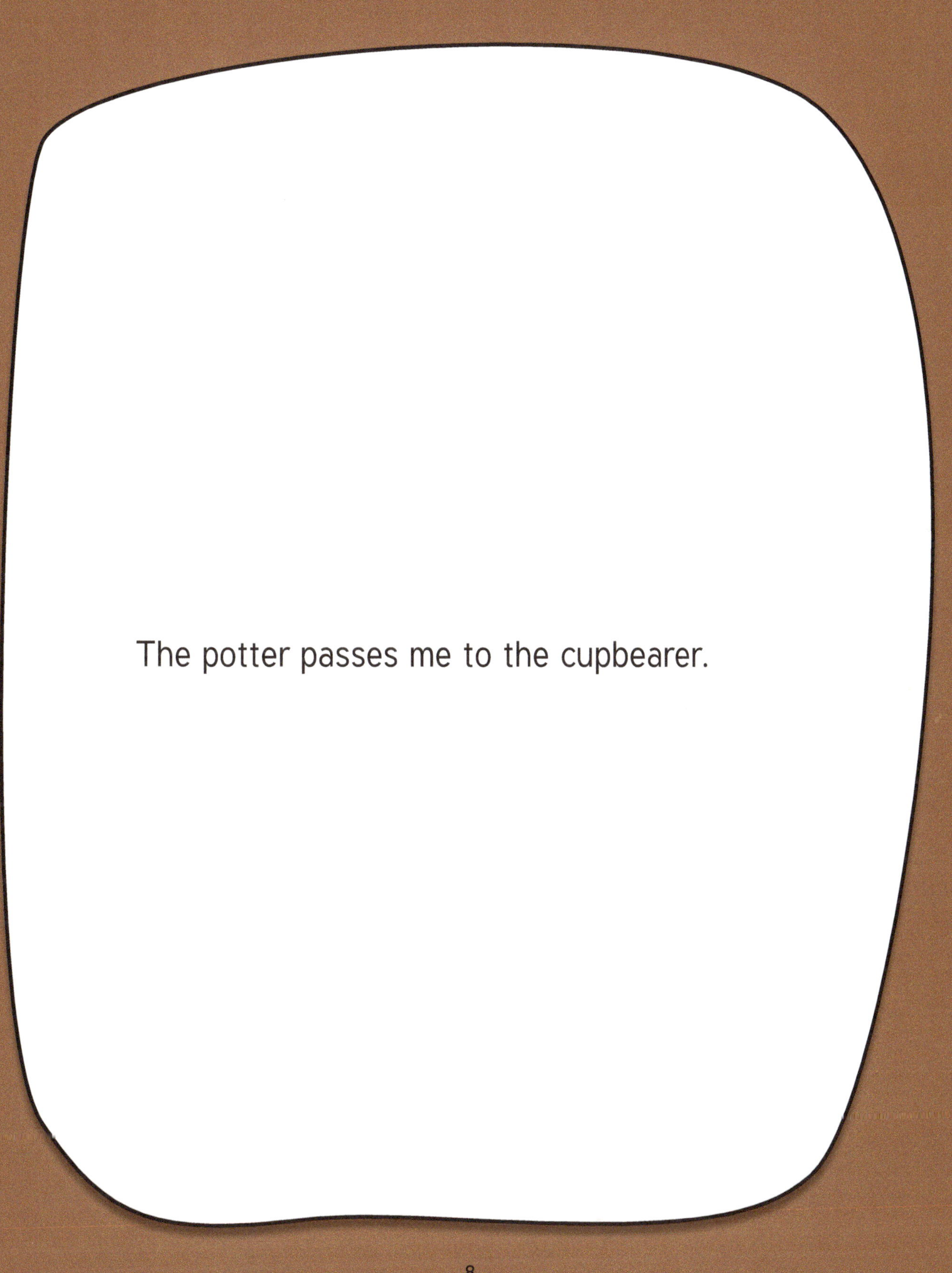

The potter passes me to the cupbearer.

There they are, all the other cups. They stood tall made of gold, shining from every angle, covered in beautiful colorful rubies.

I introduce myself, only for them to all be too proud to speak to me.

They said they couldn't speak to me because today was the day one of them would be picked to be the goblet in the Master's hand.

They told me to go back to the old barn where the potter made me because there would be no way the Master would choose a cup made of clay over a golden goblet.

I began to believe they were right. My maker hadn't made me as strong as the gold or as shiny or decorative as the others.

Just then the cupbearer walked in with the Master. Everyone straightened up, and I stood honored to just be in the Master's presence.

As the King looked at every cup, I saw Him look at the strong fully covered goblet in front of me. I knew it was a beautiful moment for that goblet, but wait!

The Master was not looking at the other goblets; He was looking at *me*! I tried to contain my excitement.

He reached down, picked me up, and said, "This will be my cup. He will be my vessel, and I will be his Master."

That night, I joined Him for a party called the Lamb's Feast. I got to celebrate with the Master and all His children! I loved the way He would hold me tightly when He would make a toast.

I loved the way He picked me out of all the other goblets and how He loved me just the way I was!

I can't help but think, *From the barn to the palace.* I will be His chosen vessel, and He will be my Master.

THE END

Bible Reference

This is the word that came to Jeremiah from the Lord: "Go down to the potter's house, and there I will give you my message." So I went down to the potter's house, and I saw him working at the wheel. But the pot he was shaping from the clay was marred in his hands, so the potter formed it into another pot, shaping it as seemed best to him. (Jeremiah 18:2–4)

In a large house there are articles not only of gold and silver but also of wood and clay; some are for special purposes and some for common use. (2 Timothy 2:20)

But we have this treasure in jars of clay to show that this all-surpassing power is from God and not from us. (2 Corinthians 4:7)

About the Author

 Genesis V. Salmon is the author of *The Cup in the Master's Hand.* Two of her favorite things have to be children's books and all things God. This is why this book is such a dream come true for her. For as long as she can remember, she has loved children's books. In a world full of distractions and social pressures, she loves the escape, peace, and joy reading can bring. She wants to help children fall in love with reading and help them know who they truly are in Christ.

Mrs. Salmon's prayer is to connect children with hope in Jesus Christ through His Holy Spirit. This book is a lighthearted reminder of how people should see themselves through the eyes of God and not focus on their own weakness. She believes in the power of the Holy Spirit and His power to uplift people's minds from everyday life into other realms, where anything can happen through God and His promises.

CPSIA information can be obtained
at www.ICGtesting.com
Printed in the USA
LVHW010738310523
748223LV00013B/83

9 781685 706708